To
Maureen and Den
for their tenure a
La Roche aux Moin
A very special place.

Autumn

Falling Leaves

David Gordon Rose

RoseTintedSpecs Imprint

Copyright Matters

RoseTintedSpecs Imprint
Butchers Farm, Molash, Kent, United Kingdom
www.rosetintedspecs.com
email: publisher@rosetintedspecs.com

Author/ photographer

David Gordon Rose

Autumn

Falling Leaves

Introduction

This seasonal volume **Autumn** in my Anorak's Guides features leaves in abundance, including many photographed during their fall to rest. This is not so quirky since it is this shedding of the leaves of deciduous trees indicating Nature has finished its work for the year that epitomises Autumn.

There are other indicators to the onset of the season, the search for warm gloves, rain in your face and tell-tale smoke around chimney pots. The sky is grey and heavy and the wind brisk reminding us again it is fallen and falling leaves and a steady change of colours until there are none, that shows Autumn is on its way through once again.

In the Natural World we notice shorter days, cooler nights and changeable skies before a real change in the weather. Above are sessile oaks in Poitou-Charentes and opposite, a bridge over the Montgomery Canal, Llanymynech, Wales in late September. There is but a hint of autumn colouring. It partly depends on where you are. The private lake opposite in Charente was photographed on 05 October. I was invited to take the boat out and photograph animals coming to drink but, without a hat, the sun was still merciless.

By October smaller migratory birds have made themselves scarce across Northern Europe. Larger birds, as the cranes above over Dordogne on 02 November leave it much later before their journey down the western edge of Europe to North Africa. Geese follow the coast, cranes keep inland. Sometimes they are only a week ahead of snow coming down Scandinavia. Leaves have been falling steadily for weeks all over Europe. By mid-November across France freezing mornings are taking their toll. The iced leaf in Deux-Sèvres, Central France was photographed on 19 November and the walnut grove opposite in the northern Dordogne on 24 November. Hard core Autumn is only five or so weeks out of the official twelve of September-November.

Overleaf is a tree sculpture in Kings Wood, Challock, Kent in mid-September. Compare the soft greens with the overtly autumnal feel of the double page picture following, the foot of Bulbarrow Hill, Dorset a week later, though different year. The light across the fields and red-brown hues of the bracken, bramble and woodland of Blackmore Vale will have looked

much the same 2,000 Autumns past. Atop the hill is Rawlsbury Camp. This Iron Age hillfort and Neolithic causeway passing it were already ancient when the Romans arrived. It is not fanciful to suggest all these early people will have enjoyed and benefitted from this season as we do today.

Autumn: Falling Leaves ends with a conflagration on 10 November. Even after much leaf-watching for this book and occasionally helping with their raking and disposal, leaves retain their endless fascination.

Impressed with a new camera three Autumns ago I set out to capture a perfect shot of a leaf in free fall. Even after sorting camera settings this photographer was still all over the place with the erratic trajectories. It didn't get easier with deteriorating weather. After an icy November night in 2019 and the first sunshine in ten days, I shot 1,800 pictures of cascading leaves in less than an hour for some last images for my portfolio.

Pages six and seven show what you are up against, even with big horse chesnut or plane tree leaves. Tracking them is tricky, especially with a telephoto lens. The RAW image (page 7) from the Nikon D810 was shot at f8, 500 ISO at 300 mm giving a shutter speed of 1600 secs. Because of the camera's high resolution I was able to crop and retain detail. There was luck here that light was also shining through the leaf.

Finally, a note on colour enhancement of images in the book; there isn't any, except for a reduction in the cyan in red and yellow. The eye compensates for this yellow-green blue cast from Autumn skies showing below right. Photographic film and modern cameras don't.

1. September

Autumn begins with a glimpse below of the *manoir* at La Roche aux Moines in Deux-Sèvres overlooking the Argenton river that was home to philosopher and author Marie-Madeleine Davy (1903-1998). One of France's original thinkers, Mme. Davy wrote prolifically on religious and spiritual matters. People with a sensibility to such things feel her presence in the house and along the riverside walk and probably that of her visitors and close friends. One was Simon Weil (d. 1943). Also a formidable intellect, Weil took first place in philosophy at the Sorbonne in Paris ahead of Simone de Beauvoir.

After WWII Mme. Davy refused to travel to Paris to receive a commendation for her work with the *Resistance* and escaping Allied personnel. General de Gaulle had to come to the house. She was a naturist and embraced trees naked along the river bank from when she was a child. Returning home in the late 1930s she lamented how

the terraces and paths had become overgrown. The riverside path (opposite) has recently been restored. Work on the bridge is ongoing. A distinguishing feature of the house is the star. The Davy uncle who expanded the property in the mid-19th Century was a wealthy Parisian lawyer and, it seems, a socialist.

This peaceful riverside setting is perfect for concentrating on leaves. Species abound, acacia, ash, cypress, bamboo, beech, plane and cedar, a different mix

from the oaks mainly that edge the surrounding fields of white Charolais cattle.

Every day along the river is an event. One night frost triggered the plane trees to let go of their leaves *en masse*. Tail winds of a large Atlantic low assisted over the following days. Within hours of heavy rain the water was discharging fully over both weirs, the rest flowing towards the old mill race and foaming chute. Escaping Argenton river leaves are caught on camera on pages 69, 70-71, 117 and 119.

Yviers and Champagne-et-Fontaines

Below, in Yviers in Poitou-Charentes in early September after the first rain in months and a gusty wind, a tree almost caught Simone's house. The event got the *pompiers* busy and gave the villagers a talking point.

Opposite, Pat's garden in the village and left, a crucifix in the woods by the ruins of Yviers castle (overleaf) showing beech and black ash thriving around the soft chalk walls.

Above, a friendly *bonjour* from the wisteria-festooned house by the church at Rioux-Martin, the next village to Yviers where I was photographing cemetery plaques for another Anorak's Guides volume. September 24, a T-shirt and barely a leaf has turned.

The lakeside snack bar opposite, Le Coq d'Or, is a little further north at Champagne-et-Fontaines in the northern Dordogne, *Périgord Vert*. The bar was deserted and full of leaves and a perfect place in which to pour a coffee and enjoy the stillness and silence across the water. With only an occasional passing bee, your own head generates music and conversation if you want it. There was little evidence of this unsigned recreation area having many visitors even during the August holiday season.

Many of the leaves pictured so far are early starters prompted by the parched summers of 2018 and 2019 that affected all of Europe. The following double page shows a corner of Champagne-et-Fontaines well in to October. Leaves falling in this mild corner are still largely unnoticed.

Fungi and animalia

Several things are associated with Autumn including hunting, animals fattening up prior to winter hibernation, fungi, berries, nuts and the last of the kitchen garden vegetables. This volume is concerned with leaves but animals come into their own, or perhaps are more easily seen poking around fallen leaves and along the sparser hedgerows.

Salamanders emerge from woodland on damp nights when there is a cover of leaves. Their primary, warning yellow make them highly visible even among beech leaves. Opposite is a coypu, sometimes known as the European Beaver, on the Vienne in Poitou-Charentes. These animals are prodigious feeders and strip river banks and any nearby garden of green material. The French don't eat them because of the stigma of their rat-like tail, though I have seen *terrine de ragondin avec Armagnac.* The following double page was a fungi theme park on top of the hill overlooking the village of Halse in Northamptonshire on 18 November.

CUEILLETTE
DE
CHAMPIGNONS
INTERDITE

Also in the northern Dordogne is this *pigeonier,* left, in open fields that once provided food for a *manoir* of which there is no trace. Many such buildings in France have been converted to holiday gites and thereby saved from dereliction.

As larger trees like the magnificent beeches in the Kings Forest, Challock on pages 16-17 are shedding leaves with grandeur, smaller bushes and shrubs will outdo them briefly with a brilliant array of leaves, berries, fruit and seeds.

Unless you are out noting changes, it is by stealth at September's end that trees seem suddenly bereft of cover. Colours stare at you and you are likely to scare birds busy feeding. Animal activity can be frantic. Though the proliferation of fruits and berries varies from place to place, year to year, there is usually plenty of food for animals stocking up. Early frost and a shortening of Autumn is more difficult for animals to cope with, along with destructive human activity.

2. October

A second French property featured in this book is Le Grand Theuillac in Charente-Maritime. Opposite is a corner of the main house and sundial, wine cellar, granary and well on 19 October. The preceding double page shows the distant Gironde estuary a few kilometres away. Medieval in origin LGT was the seat of administrative families and a 17th C. admiral to whom there is an obelisk in Cozes nearby. It is built on the line of a Roman road that older people remember in use as a farm track.

On the estuary is Talmont-sur-Gironde and the site of *Novioregum,* the main Roman port of entry into Western Europe. Goods from the far north-west of the empire passed through here. They were carted down the estuary to *Burdigala* (Bordeaux), crossing South-West France to the Mediterranean. In front of LGT are two magnificent lime trees of different species flowering two weeks apart. They look the same in a photograph of 1876 I am told, as my 2017 photograph on pages 62-63.

There is a sadness about properties shut up for the winter. Here are wonderful colours and seldom anyone to bask in the prettiness. Wild animals are in their element. Roe deer, *chevreuil,* forage the lawns, hares scamper in the fields. Left, is a hoopoe on the granary roof on a rare visit in April 2018. On the following page the dairy, *laiterie,* and two of the gardener's champion Braques d'Auvergnes, a breed he helped rescue from extinction in France in the 1960s.

Returning to Roche aux Moines for a moment and riverside colours. These are the yellow-green of Autumn ash (above), acacia, bamboo, beech, mistletoe and the soft red-brown carpet of needles from Lebanese cedars. The river rises with winter rains but never floods with two *barrages* and the remains of a mill race downstream. The water is turgid and turbid, opposite and overleaf at *barrage* two, reflecting the woodland colours before spilling over.

As October progresses we see the last flush of colour in trees and bushes as brighter leaves fall and the hawthorn, rosehips, cotoneaster, yew, dogwood, elderberry, bramble, honeysuckle and many other berries are scoffed.

Overleaf are olives from Charente, Normandy sloes and hawthorn berries and bryony from Britain. On pages 80-81 the limes and horse chesnut trees at LGT on 25 November showing the gardeners' serious leaf management stage has begun.

73

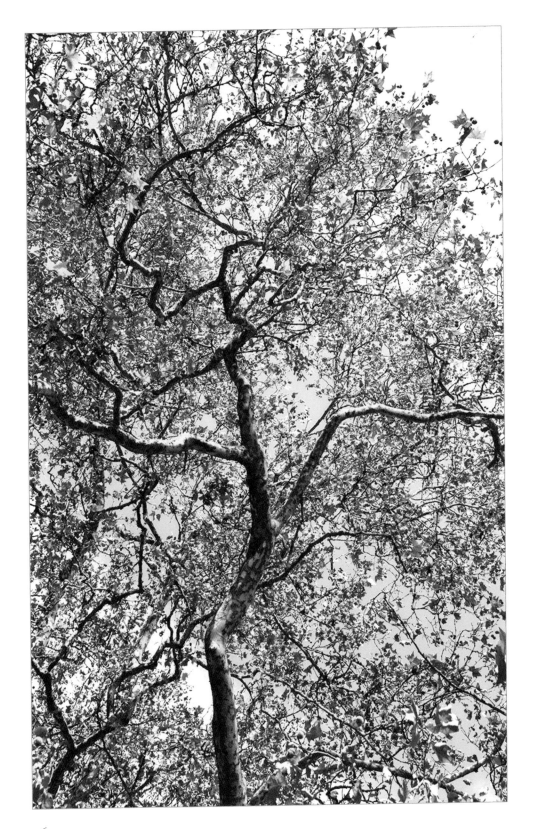

The last of the bright colours hang on to the end of the month. After much rain, mist and leaden skies, sunny days are very welcome. Bird activity has eased, apart from raucous larger blackbirds, pigeons, hawks and other birds of prey with on eye on the open fields. Animals are more visible with woodland and hedgerow having dropped its camouflage. These include deer, boar, rabbits, hare, foxes, coypou, beaver, badger and small rodents. The wait now is for the snow.

3. November

As Autumn tips towards Winter, leaves need managing. Here are several pictures of the grounds around a *Périgordine manoir,* a Dordogne manor house, that needed to be kept tidy. Ten hectares of parkland around the house presents the gardeners on duty with a thankless task from September to December. Occasionally there is a stroke of luck with a strong wind helping a leaf-blower (left) coax the leaves towards the woods.

Leaves begin falling in August from the summer heat as in the 06 September picture of the *boules* court below. It also means assistant gardeners working into the evening (pages 100-101) if the main tractor is needed for other work. Contract gardeners prefer letting leaves lie. The mulch assists weed control but it takes time in the Spring for lawns to recover. Decomposing leaves, especially with a lot of rain are at their least attractive in winter months.

One of the last trees to shed its leaves is the Ginkgo biloba. They were often planted to celebrate a birth and inspire longevity. Here, perhaps for a another reason they are by the gates at the *manoir* and La Roche aux Moines. The mature seeds are like over-ripe cherries but seriously rancid. Opposite, a grove of beech trees on an exposed hillside. Overleaf an avenue of fallen leaves and maybe a long barrow on a south-west slope in the Argenton valley that needs investigating.

Hunter and hunted

Hunting is a serious autumn-winter pastime in rural France to the extent that walkers in woods are occasionally shot at and killed. There are *chasse* signs everywhere and the barking of hunting dogs echoes around the hills on hunt days. *Palombières* (left and overleaf) are constructed for catching wood pigeons unaware. Strings animate model birds or live birds are tied to platforms to attract passers-by.

Cats are much appreciated as hunters around country properties. Above, a suspiciously well-fed semi-feral cat at the *manoir*. He was known simply as "Hello Cat." Next to him Missey in Poitou-Charentes. Right, Humphrey in Charente on a dashboard, nice and warm in the sun. Coincidentally these are all British Shorthair black and whites. Opposite, an autumnal view of Sandon in Hertfordshire and the hills of Aveyron, South-West France from a cosy living-room.

Tribute

One more tribute goes to world water speed record holders Sir Malcolm Campbell and his son Donald. Sir Malcolm broke land and water speed records several times, reaching a speed of 141 mh (228 kph) on Coniston Water in the English Lake District in 1939. His son also broke land and water speed records and met his end on the lake in January 1967 in Bluebird K7. Attempting to break his own world record he exceeded 320 mph on a second run when the craft went airborne. His remains and that of Bluebird were raised from the deep in 2001.

The lake is one of the longest (at five miles) in the Lake District and a quiet, peaceful place in Autumn, though Records Week in early November is still set aside for water speed record attempts. My picture is from 28 November, 2006. It was mild enough for deciduous trees along the bank to have retained their autumn foliage even this far north in England.

Opposite and overleaf, the Argenton river walk at the end of November after sub-zero temperatures and a week of rain. Compare the image with that taken only four weeks earlier on pages 24-25.

Different aspects of weather battle for supremacy. Six hundred miles south of Britain, France does not escape the huge Atlantic winter lows associated with what hits the British Isles though it is milder and a little sunnier.

Opposite, the evening sky of 12 November over Charente-Maritime. On a frosty morning a few days later in Dordogne, the gardener is tidying up branches and twigs at the *manoir*. Left, my last falling leaf of 2019 in Central France on 19 November.

The leaves are mostly gone. Those still to fall will be left to be devoured by bacteria and returned to Earth as those piled up in the woods or in compost bins. A few will be burnt over coming sunsets.

Printed in Poland
by Amazon Fulfillment
Poland Sp. z o.o., Wrocław

52122722R00079